REVIVING THE WORK ENVIRONMENT:

TAKING YOUR POSITION AS A LEADER

BY

JAMES SALIBA

1

REVIVING THE WORK ENVIRONMENT:

TAKING YOUR POSITION AS A LEADER

Copyright © 2020, JAMES SALIBA +

Printed in the United States of America

First Printing, 2020

Published by: James Saliba Inc., San Jose, CA   info@JamesSaliba.com

ISBN #: 978-1-7349061-0-3

Disclaimer

All the material contained in this book is provided for educational and informational purposes only. No responsibility can be taken for any results or outcomes resulting from the use of this material.

While every attempt has been made to provide information that is both accurate and effective, the author does not assume any responsibility for the accuracy or use/misuse of this information.

Some names have been changed and/or omitted in order to protect the privacy of certain individuals in this book.

For my wife Antoinette and daughters Dolores and Michelle
who continually explore leadership each in their own unique ways.
Thank you for helping me find my own vision.

"The very essence of leadership
is that you have to have a vision"
-Reverend Theodore Hesburgh, C.S.C.

TABLE OF CONTENTS

INTRODUCTION

"Think about your worst boss and pick one word to describe how that person made you feel."   Often, in my various roles as Coach, Consultant, Trainer, and Speaker, I use opportunities conversing with groups of employees across many industries.   When asking them about their worst boss and how that person made them feel, it amazes me how much they have to talk about, sharing, and comparing negative experiences.   When I turn the question around to come up with a word about their best boss, someone they would like to work with again, the conversations grow significantly less energic.

In my roles I listed above, it is my passion to grow the "best boss" conversation to be the louder and more energetic discussion. At the same time, these best bosses, these "Leaders" must build business success and personal fulfillment.

From brand new to decades of experience, all Leaders can find themselves "stuck" at times. And often, this "stuck" is stopping progress, and the "stuck" isn't even an issue or problem that is worthwhile attempting to fix. The value of the repair is less than the value of moving on.

Leadership presupposes success; Leaders are perceived to be role models. In the business or work environment, you, the Leader, are sometimes faced with insurmountable challenges that threaten the organization. The secret to overcoming these obstacles is your ability to follow business principles in three simple pillars, making your business and career skyrocket to success.

This book is divided into these three pillars, as they are called here. By taking contemplative time to assess yourself, then assessing overall performance, and then taking the appropriate actions, you will move forward at hyper speed. This isn't just a 'read me' book; there are numerous exercises embedded throughout to allow you to reflect on your work and progress, to build a path for you to do that hyper speed movement.

The first pillar is YOU. No one handles a business as professionally as the person who has made all the sacrifices and comes to a position of leadership, whether first line or C Level. When you have come to a proper understanding of your reality, you become cognizant of your mission, values, and vision. The work and success you require IS within you!

How well do you know your work performance? The competition surrounding your work environment is an avenue for you to create a difference. As you move through this book, you will assess your performance as well as the key initiatives behind your business venture. That is, your motivating factors. In this way, if and when other things do not always proceed as planned, your motivation keeps you going. Additionally, you create and build sustainable relationships in your work environment. Between your motivation and your relationships, your performance pillar should hold firm.

After all is in place, the third pillar is, taking action! Bring your vision and mission into reality. The quest for success comes with continuous learning. So, brace yourself to acquire professional development actions. Embrace feedback from your work environment and put it into action. In simple terms, as you act, take note of what is working and what is not. Assess why and how it can be improved. This constant action/assessment/repeat process is how companies move forward, and often well ahead of any competition.

Undoubtedly, no work environment thrives when the employees are dissatisfied with the Leaders. As well, dissatisfaction from other sources, a morale issue based on the company's environmental position, or simply permitting too much sun on staff desks during the day… it is the Leader's job and responsibility to inspire individuals and increase their willingness to play their part within the team structure to succeed. Teamwork is important regardless of who is referred to as the team Leader. It is the willingness of all individuals to play their part in the organization that determines its success rate. Therefore, it is essential the organizational morale is at its peak. And, not in a rah-rah way that excites and then dissipates within the day way, but in a long term, understanding of the company's goals and mission, exciting the team to move with these goals and mission and exercise actions that promote those goals and mission, way.

Sometimes, Leaders pay more attention to the changing demands of the market and seek ways to meet the demands of their ever-rising audience. In doing this, they fail to realize their employees are also in dire need of their presence as a Leader, and abandon them to pursue other issues they consider more relevant at the specific moment. More so, they fail to keep abreast of the aspects of the work environment that are sacrosanct, such as vision, mission, performance, and how to become effective in the long run. Without these missions and goals, the direction of the company falters, and much harder and faster if the leadership is focused elsewhere.

No doubt, a majority of Leaders want to create a favorable, motivated atmosphere for their employees to work, but for certain reasons, they may not be able to achieve such an environment. The employees, on the other hand, may not really understand the efforts the Leaders are putting into place and may lose interest in the job. This is a constant balancing act; keep morale to the mission in a positive and 'real' way, and without creating automaton-like staff responses or actions.

In all, being a Leader requires patience, skills, and dedication. A Leader must be able to juggle different activities at the same time and successfully create a balance without paying attention to a certain area and ignoring another. It is when a Leader attains this level, such a person is considered to have overcome the hurdles.

While this seems like an impossible business conundrum to resolve, being a Leader is not beyond the capacity of ordinary humans. The first things to recognize are your abilities and strengths. It is only when you pay close attention to various leadership styles that you will realize how to work in line with the style that suits you the most, and more importantly, achieve your desired result.

This book contains detailed steps to serve as a guide to help you revive your business and assume your position as the Leader you are. Your questions, fears, and doubts are adequately discussed to ensure you achieve your goals and mission. It is an all-encompassing book that helps you navigate your way and come to a favorable, profitable, successful end.

PILLAR ONE

GETTING TO KNOW YOURSELF

GETTING TO KNOW YOURSELF

Getting to know yourself is the first pillar of success. And, as much as you might believe you know yourself, this is often the first stumbling block to success. This is the most important section of the book in this respect. DO NOT gloss over it, or simply say you don't need to do this, or you have taken tests before and know all your own strengths and weaknesses. If you really knew all this, we wouldn't be here. If you plan on following the program and succeeding at the program... then be a part of the program... focus on how to achieve the program... then, DO the program!

You may have tried virtually everything you know, by the book, to ensure you are creating a difference. Yet, nothing seems to work. It is understandable for you to feel upset and devastated at the outcome of the situation especially when you have done everything within your power to make things work. But, there may be something you have not yet tried. Yes! You don't know yourself well enough to bring about the results you expect.

So many times, you find out that your employees, colleagues, or even partners, do not go along with you. It is not because they do not respect your stance or want the best for you. It is simply because you have failed to understand your personality and work in that direction. It is only when you identify with your own makeup that these things become easier for you.

The reality of your personality stares you in the face at every given turn, but sometimes you fail to see it. You can achieve much if you come to terms with your personality and your leadership style. More so, you will experience less pushback, less resistance, when you are able to accept the reality of who you are. Your personality affects everything about and around you, and the stress to do well, achieve, and perform to your best level, is especially true in the work environment. This is why it is very important to come to terms with its presence. Otherwise, your mission, vision, performance, and work environment will be affected negatively.

There are various personality and leadership styles. To ascertain your personality type, you can take an assessment online. It will move you in the right direction and make you better at everything you work to achieve in your business.

Remember, the problem is often your personal values are not in alignment with your corporate mission and goals. How can that be, you say? It is MY company, MY department, MY team... of course it reflects MY values. Unfortunately, unless you know what you are made of, what makes you tick, you will never know if you, your company, your department, or team, are on the same path.

I cannot strongly suggest enough, recommend, even demand, you take a personality test... a serious personality test, not one on the back of a cereal box, and discover everything you can about yourself. How can you fix what you don't understand?

This is Job #1. Do it today, tomorrow at the latest.

❖ **Some of the better known personality assessments are:**

Myers Briggs personality test: As a leader in an organization, it is critical you understand your personality type. While this may seem to be of little or no importance to you, the success rate of your organization greatly depends on it. How do you analyze situations in the work place? Are you judgmental in dealing with your employees and partners? How do you react when you cannot control the things around you? These questions are issues that stare you in the face at the workplace. No matter how hard you try, they just keep coming back. Taking the personality test is a stepping stone to making progress at work.

This Myers Briggs assessment is based on relationships and the ability to work with various energy levels. In this assessment, there are sixteen personality types. The Myers Briggs test examines the attitude of individuals in exerting energies. When taking this test, you (as the test taker) understand if you want to channel your energy to ideas and information or would prefer to deal with people and things.

Another part of the Myers Briggs personality test examines how you process information. That is, if you like to understand the facts clearly before making a decision, or if you will accept and deal with the results of the unknown. The third part of the personality test analyzes the way you make use of your senses, or would rather settle for intuition. The fourth part of the Myers Briggs personality test analyzes the choice of lifestyle you adopt. In this last part of the personality test, you will be able to ascertain if you prefer to live your life in a planned manner or would rather prefer to go with the flow with no plan whatsoever.

The Myers test can be taken online, free. When you take this test, it helps you determine the type of career and leadership position that suits you best. At this writing, here is a link for you to take the test: https://www.16personalities.com/free-personality-test

Wheel of Life: The Wheel of Life is a personality assessment that measures the various aspects of your life. It examines those aspects with the idea of discovering what is out of balance and requires attention or improvement. These include the relationships you keep with the individuals around you. Relationships are inarguably very important for personal growth. But, there are also some relationships that may cause damage to your life if adequate care is not taken with them.

The Wheel presumes we are all one person regardless of our many hats. We are parents and children. We are siblings and relatives. We are worker and boss, leader and helper, all at once, and all the time. Whenever we are out of balance, the Wheel can help identify the issue and stop the friction slowing everything else down. The Wheel of Life test helps to examine factors at play in your life you consider important. This can include; fun, money, friends, spirituality, career, love, and health. With the aid of the Wheel of Life test, you will have knowledge of the various aspects of your life that are flourishing and the areas that need work either somewhat slightly or very seriously.

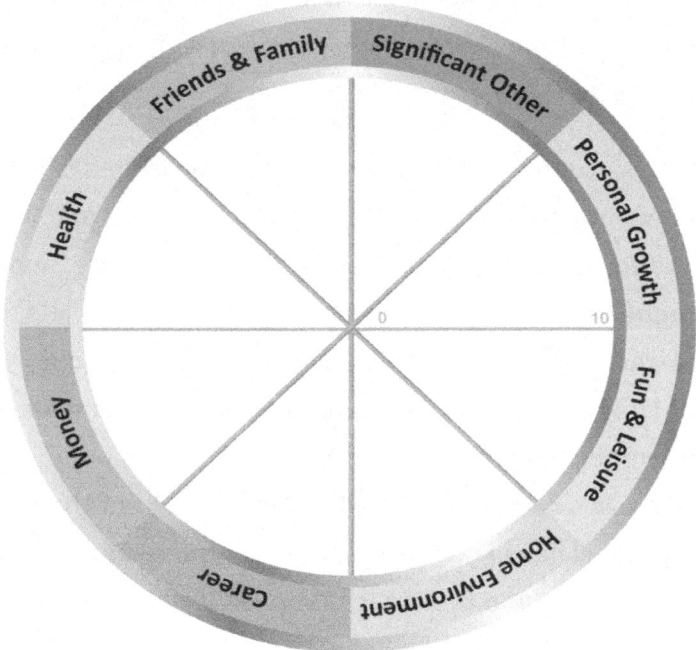

The appropriate exercises that go with the Wheel of Life may be found in the Appendix of the book.

❖ Leadership Styles

There are various leadership styles. As an individual, you may be required to lead a certain group of people. It could be in your family, at work, school, or even in your religious organization. When such responsibility is handed over to you, what helps you create a long-lasting impact is the knowledge of the type of leader you are.

It is important to understand a bit of background. The 'style' of leadership in organizations and companies goes back to the early 1900s when we began to have the modern-day organization and company. And, back in that time, workers truly were workers, often without much education, and the work was manual; management people were more educated, and their work was more cerebral. Today, most of the workers in corporate environments are fairly educated all the way to substantially overeducated knowledge workers. It makes little sense we are using over 100 year old leadership methods to lead a completely different category of 'worker' over 100 years later.

I strongly believe that no matter your leadership style, being authentic in leadership is the key to understanding and leading in all organizations today. This doesn't mean we ignore other styles, we just use them more effectively within the style we have chosen.

Your leadership style reveals much about you. It is the manner in which you make decisions, implement those decisions, and motivate the people around you.

There are basically three leadership styles. Each of these styles has at least one or more "sub-categories" of styles, but we will not be getting into that detail in this book. By knowing which style we tend to "go to" most often, it is helpful for our understanding of ourselves as leaders. We could use them all, but we do tend to "go to" one in particular when we need help.

Developing an 'authentic leadership style', which is one of the keys to leadership success, requires us to understand and know our personalities and combine that with our preferred leadership style. This begins to create the 'authentic' in authentic leadership since it comes from inside.

The three general leadership styles are:

Autocratic leadership style: This type of leadership style is a unilateral direction. The leader gives out orders and instructions and doesn't depend on the feedback of his/her subordinates. That is, the leader doesn't want the opinion or suggestion of his followers. This type of leadership style is best when the leader has a short time to deliver a certain task or has the available information for the job at his/her disposal. Autocratic leadership style doesn't mean using abusive words or demeaning language to direct subordinates. This style of leadership should not be used at all times.

Participative leadership style: This type of leadership style involves the participation of the subordinates or followers. The leader who uses this leadership style acknowledges the presence of her/his subordinates and would ask their opinion on certain issues. Nonetheless, the leader still makes the final decision. For the participative leadership style, the leader has some information at his disposal and his subordinates are also in possession of valuable information. Thus, both parties have to work together to achieve results. This is the best form of leadership as it makes the employees feel respected and part of the organization or assigned duty. Transformational, democratic, and charismatic styles are all sub categories of this style.

Laissez-faire leadership style: In this leadership style, the leaders permit the employees to make decisions based on a trust basis. But, the leader takes responsibility for the decisions the employees or subordinates make. Before a leader adopts this leadership style, s/he needs to ascertain the employees/subordinates are capable of analyzing the situation and generating meaningful results.

This is a continuum, with Autocratic on one side, where the leader makes all the decisions with no input from team, to a Laissez-faire on the other side, where the leader allows the team to make most of the decisions without input for the leader. All the other participative styles are spread in the middle.

Exercise: In the two charts below, fill in the results of your testing and your personal comments about the results. Then, in the second, note your reaction to the results and one example of these categories in your personal daily life. DO NOT SKIP THIS EXERCISE AT RISK OF LOSS OF TEAM, DEPARTMENT, AUTHORITY, OR COMPANY.

	Write in results	Personal comments
Personality type		
Leadership type		
Top 2 or 3 Wheel of Life categories you would like to improve		

	Reaction to Result	One Example in Your Daily Life
Personality type		
Leadership type		
Top 2 or 3 Wheel of Life categories you would like to improve		

VISION

A Vision is the foundation of leadership.

Many employees and even mid and upper management believe the Vision is the job of the CEO. In my opinion, they are wrong. Everyone needs to have a Vision.

A Vision for yourself: Your career, personal life, and personal goals.

A Vision for your team or department: How your team is working together, or, how your department is going to reach this or that goal by the end of the year.

So many in corporate middle management ignore this need. They expect the Visions to come down from high, on a corporate wide basis, like an umbrella, covering them and their work and department as well. These will be the first middle management people to lose their positions. Being told what to do is NOT a leadership characteristic!

Let me restate for clarity and to re-emphasize this critical point: EVERYONE needs to have a Vision... from front line staff to C level executives.

Casting a clear Vision tells your employees or associates where they'll be if they join, work, and grow with you and your team, department, and company. If you want to craft a powerful Vision, first ask, what will your life or your organization look like when you reach your vision? What does success look like? What are we aspiring to achieve?

Guide your "Vision Discussion" session along with these tips:

- Start with "We envision…"
- Use the future tense, as if you are already there.
- Plan on making your vision obsolete within a year, ready to reassess and start again.

Find the healthy tension between aspirational and magical thinking. You want a statement that inspires and motivates, but that is also based in reality.

Sidebar: In my experience, many leaders struggle with the concept of thinking "into the future". A long term plan is simply too much to comprehend, particularly in this day of the world moving at hyper speed. So, as a leader, you might want to not only provide this Vision, but also some simpler, closer 'sub-visions':

- In the next three months…
- In the next six months…
- In the next year…

Every leader needs a Vision. It is only when the Vision is in place the leader aligns himself to making efforts that causes him to stand out in the crowd. The Vision helps leaders stay focused and not drift away in unfavorable circumstances.

It is when the Vision is clear and attainable the leader makes the right kind of decisions, leading to the Vision. The choice of a leader's Vision reveals the type of person s/he is and it affects the individuals around her/him. When people are convinced or motivated about your choice of vision, they find it easy to work with you and help you reach your goal. For this reason, it is pertinent every leader's Vision must possess some specific characteristics.

➢ These characteristics include:

Motivating factor: The Vision needs to be captivating. You need to model your Vision in a way that shows your plan for the future. This would explain you are not solely concerned about the present or past but are focusing on the possibilities of the future. This also includes not being 100% focused on profits but on people, progress, and benefit to society. When your Vision speaks volumes of the future and greater positivity, there will be many individuals who will indicate interest in working with you, because of your choice of Vision.

Positive image: There are many benefits to being positive. Your Vision should have a positive outlook, ALWAYS. Even if the future does not look very bright, there is no reason to dwell on it. Yes, speak to it, and then speak to better things. It is simply not enough for your Vision to motivate others. It also needs to create a lasting impression on as many of those who hear it. What do you hope to give to those employees who buy into your Vision? Remember, many staff are interested in your Vision because they are motivated by it. But, what do they stand to gain? You need to describe this in the simplest way possible! Positive and inclusive of everyone.

Possibility: Your Vision should be achievable, challenging, or audacious, but most importantly it should be achievable. Inasmuch as you have presented your Vision in a positive image, it is also important you help bring the Vision to life. When you have a Vision that looks far-fetched, the motivating factor to bring it to life becomes difficult. An unrealistic Vision may not be achievable and can minimize the motivation needed to accomplish it. In drafting the Vision for your organization or department, it should have many elements of possibility.

There are various examples of Visions. It may be a personal Vision, organizational Vision, departmental Vision, or even a team Vision. Before you define or build departmental, team, or organizational Vision, you need to create a personal Vision. Your personal Vision serves as a guide to help you create all the other Visions you use.

The below questions will take you on a path of self-discovery. It is important you answer these questions in all honesty. It prepares you for an in-depth understanding of who you are, how to maximize your strengths, and work on your weaknesses.

An example of a personal Vision is: Through socializing with individuals, I will become more informed and acquire the needed skills to make me a better person. My love for reading and writing will be put to good use by affecting society positively and creating awareness on the importance of literature. I will love everyone I come in contact with and teach people how to love, because I am aware that giving love comes with responsibility. I prefer putting my effort into whatever I set out to do and will not rest on my laurels until I achieve my goal.

Worksheet for personal vision

	List three examples on these columns	List one example that you regard as most important
What do I enjoy doing the most?		
Am I an extrovert or introvert?		
What are my strengths?		
How do I go about actualizing my plans?		
Am I independent or dependent on people?		
What are my values?		

In the same vein, in creating a Vision for your organization, you also need to ask questions that revolve around the organization, department, or team you lead.

The below questions are a simple guide to helping you draw a good organizational Vision. Your audience is interested in the kind of Vision your company believes. So, your team, or department, or even company's Vision is your first selling point. Before your audience comes in contact with your services or products, they are very keen on understanding the kind of Vision your organization has. Organizational Vision portrays the company in a positive or negative light. So, it is paramount to have good organization Visions that make it easy for your target audience to buy into your dreams and support your organization.

As a leader who wants the very best for the organization, it is very important you answer the below questions in the sincerest way possible. While answering the questions, if you find a question you have no clue about, it is an eye-opener you haven't been doing things the right way. It is also an avenue for you to put yourself back on the right track.

Most importantly, while creating the organizational Vision, it is also necessary you create a Vision that is in line with the industry in which you operate. That is, if your organization is rooted in the manufacturing industry, your organizational Vision must be in line with the industry. It makes your audience understand you are aware of their needs and willing to provide the right type of solution.

Your Vision also needs to have **'the human element'.** This means the Vision you create for your company shouldn't be abstract. It should be constructed in a way that expresses a connection with your audience. Your target audience needs to understand the organization has its satisfaction in mind.

Worksheet for organizational vision

Questions	Answers
What are the aims of your organization?	

How do you hope to create a difference in society? Any unique strength that sets you apart from competitors?	
Any achievements?	
What are your organizational values?	

Here is an example for more, long term, Vision thinking:

Question	3-5 years
What problem are you solving in the market?	
What products and services do you provide?	

What does your organization do better than any other? What is your organization famous for?	
Which types of customers does your organization serve? Which types doesn't it serve?	
What value does your organization provide for these customers? What is unique about the way in which you do business?	
What processes, technologies, expertise, people, and systems facilitate your Vision?	
What are the key milestones you need to reach to achieve your Vision. What major	

achievements will you celebrate along the way?	

The best way for you to understand Vision statements is for you to look at the statements made public by large corporations. While they are not always on target, most often they DO express all the points of solid Visions and should be reviewed for their successful expressions of Visions. SO, take the time to read over a number of large corporation Vision statements.

Now below, it is time for you to create your own Vision statements.

This is not a five minute project, nor a one-time project. Prepare them both. Come back to them. Redo them. Re-read the above points and make sure you are motivating yourself, and others, to higher levels of achievement.

Your personal Vision statement:

Your organizational Vision statement:

MISSION

People often confuse the difference between a Vision and a Mission, at every level of an organization. Why do you exist? The answer you provide explains your vision. Now, how are you going to accomplish that vision? THIS is the Mission. Everyone has a Mission and that includes you. In the same vein, there must be a propelling need or reason that pushes you to start up a business venture, right? That factor or motive behind your interest or passion for starting up a business venture is your Mission.

Within an organization, each team, each department, has its own Mission, whether to keep shipping errors to zero, to create a Million dollars in revenues in the Sales Department, or create an amazing catalog every year.

Missions are undeniably important for the success of the work environment. If you are to understand the reason or passion behind your chosen career path or work environment, now is the time for you to reevaluate yourself. It is erroneous to live life or start up a business venture without any propelling factor. It could be as little as the love of humanity or the desire to create a difference in society. In the work environment, the choice of an organization's Mission reveals the type of products and services it offers and its target audience as well.

Suffice to say, the organizational Mission is a statement that provides direction for an organization. The organizational Mission is primarily generated through a careful analysis of the environment and the prevailing factors. When an organizational Mission is in place, it is easy for the employees, the management team, and the leaders, to work in line with the Mission and ensure they accomplish the company's goals. The Mission clearly spells out what the company expects to achieve. This helps every team member work toward this direction in his/her own department and even at the team level.

The Mission is the singular reason for which something exists. Without the Mission, there will be no room for the continuation of the organization, and it will lead to the extinction of passion, and of the organization itself. Passion is fueled by a Mission. So, it is no surprise when your passion becomes non-existent when lacking direction to which you should move.

> **The importance of a Mission**

In every facet of life, the place of the Mission should not be underestimated. A majority of individuals who go about life without any direction of what they hope to achieve, end up with little or no result. But, when you take a close look at individuals and leaders who have left their footprints on the sands of time, one thing is always certain: purpose. They understand what they hope to get from life and, as such, channel themselves in that direction.

So, it is evident that Mission in your everyday life and in the work environment gives you a clearer path and helps you achieve a result in the shortest time possible.

Some important points of the Mission are:

- It gives the organization the needed direction to achieve its aims and objectives.

  With a Mission in place, the efforts, actions, and activities of an individual or team are channeled towards achieving targets and making the right type of decisions that makes achievement possible.

- For an organization, a Mission helps to ensure resources are allocated in the right way. When resources are evenly distributed within the organization, it helps the managers/leaders ascertain how to distribute resources so as to achieve efficiency and output in the organization.

- Additionally, the organizational Mission also creates specific job descriptions. That is, the job descriptions will be tailored in the right way, aimed at bringing about the right decisions and maximum effectiveness.

For an individual, Missions help to make passion clearer. When there is a Mission in place, it is easy for passion to be put to good use.

➤ **Questions to ask yourself**

So long as you exist, you need to evaluate yourself from time to time. The reason is very simple. Humans are social beings and we learn every day. In defining your Mission, ask yourself the following questions:

- How do I set my plans in motion?

You probably have an idea, but don't know how to go about it. It is important to identify the options at your disposal. Then, explore these options and see what works best for you.

- Am I experiencing any satisfaction in what I am doing now?

This question helps you understand if you are on the right path or not. And if your answer is no, you need to find out what creates internal satisfaction and go after it.

- What drives me?

There is always a driving force behind every action or decision you take. Ensure you discover what drives you and let it be for good reasons.

- What do I hope to achieve in my chosen path?

This is where your passion comes into play. Whatever you find yourself doing; you are doing it for a reason. There is something that pushes you to that path. But, if there is none, look again! You probably are not doing it the right way or for the right reasons.

- Where do I go from here?

This question keeps you in check at all times. Even when you are tempted to deviate from your plan, you remember you started for a reason, because there is a destination. The image of the bigger picture you have painted of yourself helps keep on the right track. More so, it also reveals the dreams to progress and become better.

Asking yourself the necessary questions makes it easy to stay firm and rooted in your mission. By so doing, you find it easy to work in line with your Mission, which serves as a guide, and makes it possible for you to set your passion to work and channel energy in your given direction.

➤ **Worksheet for developing organizational mission**

Exercise one: In less than three sentences, write out what impact the organization hopes to create and who it hopes to impact.

```
┌─────────────────────────────────────────────┐
│                                             │
│                                             │
│                                             │
│                                             │
│                                             │
└─────────────────────────────────────────────┘
```

Exercise two: What are the factors you will put into place to help the organization come to its expected result?

```
┌─────────────────────────────────────────────┐
│                                             │
│                                             │
│                                             │
│                                             │
└─────────────────────────────────────────────┘
```

Exercise three: Are there any plans for the future? An expansion? If yes, how do you intend to arrive at that point?

```
┌─────────────────────────────────────────────┐
│                                             │
│                                             │
│                                             │
└─────────────────────────────────────────────┘
```

An example of an organizational Mission: The Company exists so as to provide healthy meals to the members of the society. We are aware that eating healthy is important and as such desire to ensure that everyone eats right.

VALUES

What do you hold in high esteem? There must be something you are unwilling to compromise for anything in the world. It is something you treasure above every other thing and you structure everything you do in a way that permits you to continue to honor that Value.

In a layman's understanding, Values are principles that are treasured above all. They represent the decisions and choices you have made in life. Your Values are adequately represented in the work environment, your personal affairs, and relationships with all. Values are what matter to you the most. They are intricate aspects of your makeup you do not take for granted. It is essential for everyone to establish Values for themselves. Your Values are your standards. The individuals with whom you interact will give you respect because of how you have portrayed yourself.

Values signify your personal decision to stand out from the crowd. It is your conscious effort to be something better and remarkable. The interesting thing about having Values in your personal life or work environment is that a majority of individuals may not agree with your Values, especially when you refuse to give in to the pressure around you. But, one remarkable fact about Values is that they speak for you in the long run. Even when you are not appreciated, the success of your business, work, career path, or personal life, will depend on how you uphold your Values.

Your Values could be transparency, quality, competence, and results oriented. As long as your Values are very important to you, do not give in to the pressure around you. The benefits of Values are sometimes not immediate, but one thing is certain, having them surely pays off! So, never relent or be discouraged. You will reap the reward for upholding your Values. It could be in your business environment, personal life, or workplace. Don't be discouraged, uphold them, and they will reward always reward you.

What do Values represent in the workplace? Values in the workplace mean your work ethics and principles in the work environment. The office environment is characterized by multiple unhealthy practices. But, if you find yourself in such an environment and refuse to give in to the pressure, then you are certain to have overcome the pressures in the work environment. In such a situation, you are said to be upholding your Values in the work environment without compromise.

> **Personal and work Values**

Your personal Values are not the same as your work Values, though they certainly can be. This is because the work environment is nothing close to how you have structured your personal life. When you decide to incorporate your personal Values into your work environment, it may alter the smooth operations of your work and vice versa. So, it is necessary to separate your personal Values from your work Values; so you don't do the right things, but at the wrong place.

> **How do you align personal and work Values?**

Some examples of work Values are honesty, hard work, and attention to detail. In the work environment, you may discover some of your colleagues at work agree with some of the Values you uphold. They support the manner in which you pay attention to work and how you are transparent in your dealings. Yet, when you fail to prioritize your work Values and they may clash with one another, leading to issues in the work environment. So, the right way to handle your work Values is to learn how to prioritize.

The best way to manage your work Values so as not to encounter problems is to select work Values that are closely related to each other. When your top work Values walk hand-in-hand, you will discover there will be no room for any clash whatsoever. For example, if your work Values are discipline, integrity, and attention to detail, you wouldn't experience any issue at all in managing your work Values. This is simply because when discipline is in place, you would certainly uphold your integrity at all times, and pay attention to detail. So, there wouldn't be any clash among your work Values.

It is important to have personal Values, but you need to ensure, in the work environment, your personal Values do not impact productivity and performance. The work environment is totally different from personal activities. Failure to understand the differences in both environments can result in issues.

➢ **Values worksheet 1**

Values are principles or standards that are your guideposts for action. Using the following questions, it is time to identify your Values and the ones you consider your top priorities.

- Exercise one: Have you ever been so caught up in any activity/exercise that you lost track of time? What activity was it?

- Exercise two: What do you consider to be very useful and relevant? This could be emotions, ideals, or personal beliefs.
- Exercise three: What are the Values you hold in high esteem? List as many Values as possible and in no particular order. The appendix section has over 200 examples of Values from which you can choose.
- Exercise four: Now that you have listed your various work and personal Values, list the top ten Values (on the combined list) in no particular order.
- Exercise five: In the previous exercise, you listed ten Values. Now list your top five Values, from most favored to least favored.

➢ **Putting Values into action**

Actions are words when they are used in an appropriate manner. It is always good to prioritize your Values so you are able to put them into good use in guiding your performance. Putting your Values into action requires conscious effort. This is because there are bound to be circumstances that may cause you to want to have a change of heart.

There are two types of Values: Those you say you have and put into action, and those you say you have and don't put into action. If your actions don't match the Values you claim to embrace, then you should not call them your Values.

However, you goal is to put your Values into action. You can do this by making up your mind irrespective of the situations around you. When you put your Values into action, you will definitely get the best from the situations around you. Your Values can be put into use in your work environment or in your personal life. Whatever the case, do not let your Values become dormant because of the demands of society, work, family, or other pressures. Your environment or society may not encourage your Values. Don't let that dismay you from doing what is right and good.

In the below table fill in your values. Feel free to write out as many as possible. In the second column list reasons why the value you have chosen is indeed a value. That is, provide supporting evidence that proves what you have mentioned in the first column is a value. You've got this!

Examples of Values:

- Competence in place of friendship
- Quality in place of money
- Responsibility in place of waywardness
- Integrity in place of lies
- Carefulness in place of carelessness

Values worksheet

Values	Evidence (Actions that prove this is a Value)

PILLAR TWO

"With these special glasses,
we can all see performance is great!"

PERFORMANCE

Performance is defined as how an individual produces a result at whatever s/he sets out to do, and often, versus how others have similarly done the same task. Performance is not only based on tangible things. It also includes intangible things such as the ability to communicate effectively, efficiently, and clearly.

One thing that distinguishes one individual from another in the work environment is performance. While there may many people working in an organization, it is surprising to see only a few are interested in yielding productive results for the organization. Often the managerial team looks out for individuals who go the extra mile to bring results. When an employee is always looking for a means to do something different that will produce a result for an organization, such an employee is bound to be rewarded. Frequently, the employee may be given the opportunity to lead a group of staff in the company.

Ideally, it is in the organization's best interest to motivate employees to do their best work all the time. There are quite a number of ways the managerial team in organizations measure performance; being able to measure performance is of utmost importance. When there is no means for measuring performance, the employees will not be encouraged to put in their premier effort and time in carrying out their job duties. This is likely going to affect the organization in a negative way.

There are various types of performance at work. They include: decision making, customer satisfaction, leadership, effective communication, generating revenue, professionalism, and more.

> **Performance goals**

When you set out to do a particular task or job, you are encouraged by your goals and aims. Performance goals are usually based on a short term period. Performance goals are like a road map that helps you to prioritize your activities, and keeps you focused on important aspects and areas in the work environment. They are very specific and help you in actualizing whatever job or task is assigned to you.

In setting your performance goals, avoid ambiguous or unrealistic goals. Rather, settle for goals easily and clearly defined. It will help you in your quest to achieve results.

Are you aiming for a certain position in the organization? Do you want to get a promotion in the company? If your answer is yes, then it is time to set your performance goals.

The easiest and fastest way to get to any leadership position is to set performance goals for yourself. When you do this, you wave off distraction and channel your energy into getting the very best from your efforts. It is not just enough to aim for enviable positions; you also need to prepare mentally for the position you are aiming for. And doing this means you have to set performance goals.

> **Be SMART**

In attaining your performance goals, you must be SMART. Sometimes, you may desire to get things done in the shortest possible time, but ironically, the reverse may just be the case.

SMART is an acronym that represents:

Specific

Measurable

Articulate

Reliable

Time-sensitive

S-Specific: You may have too many things you hope to achieve in a given period of time. But, when you look at them closely, you will realize there are some tasks more important than others. What do you do? Tailor your job duties and tasks in the simplest way possible. What do you want to achieve in one week? Pay attention to it, get it done, and move on to the next task. When you want to do everything at the same time, you realize you will end up doing little or nothing.

M-Measurable: Your performance must be measurable. When going about your duties, you must ensure you understand what you are doing and the outcome that is expected. When there is an expected outcome/result, it keeps you on track, makes you focused and eliminates deviation from the original chosen path.

A-Articulate: Spell out your duties and goals clearly. Your performance may not be easy to measure when it is poorly articulated. Make it readable and accessible for yourself. Keep it in a place where you will be able to access it whenever the need arises.

R-Reliable- Don't build castles in the air when setting your performance goals. Your performance goals should be made in a reliable way. When it is reliable, it is easy to achieve. Ensure you set performance goals that are easy for you to achieve.

T-Time-sensitive: Remember, you don't have forever to set or achieve your goals. Set the time and give yourself a particular time frame to achieve your goal. When setting performance goals, ensure you give yourself a deadline. Giving yourself such a time limit helps you reach the performance goal on or before the expected time.

> ➤ **How do YOU define performance?**

As an individual, what does performance mean to you? What do you achieve that makes you feel fulfilled or satisfied? When you get to that point and can look back and beat your chest and give a proud smile, you have experienced satisfaction in whatever you find yourself doing.

Performance can come from anything you set your mind to do. It may not be easy. It has never been easy to set or achieve performance goals. But, with the right attitude, discipline, and patience, you can reach whatever performance goals you have set for yourself. All that is required is a commitment to them and to decide what is best for you. Give yourself a motivation if it makes you feel better. Perhaps, you are hoping to get a new house when you get promoted at work. It should be reason enough to help you stay focused and attain your goal in the work environment.

➢ Performance worksheet

Would you like to know how well you are faring in the position in the company? Then, this worksheet will help you determine the levels you have attained or propel you to put in more effort and get better in achieving your goals.

My Top Three Performance Goals
1
2
3

Performance worksheet and examples:

- Enroll 700 students in classes this school year.
- Increase revenue from $10 million to $13 million by the end of this fiscal year.
- Develop and beta test two new software programs, one by July 31 and one by October 31
- Hire seven additional engineers in the next three months.
- Develop a retainer relationship with five of the 50 largest companies in the Chicago area.

KEY INITIATIVES

Key initiatives are also known as strategic initiatives. They refer to actions and activities that are aimed at actualizing set goals and objectives. These initiatives are not the same as the everyday routines you go through. The initiative requires conscious effort and determination to help you reach all you hope to achieve.

The key initiatives serve as a guide to present organizations or individuals with the needed direction to achieving set goals and objectives.

➢ **Choosing your key initiatives**

No doubt, it is often difficult to choose key initiatives, especially when you have too many ideas at the same time. The first step to help in your decision making is to define what you need, and then prioritize the objectives.

After prioritizing the objectives, make certain each objective is in line with your goals and vision that we set in earlier exercises. Now think about grouping work together in obtaining these objectives. Each one of these groupings of work we can call an initiative.

Ensure you make use of the right strategy for the implementation for each of the initiatives. The fact it looks good doesn't mean it is actually good. So, be careful in selecting a strategy.

What do you need to do to make sure the key initiatives come through? Do it! Put a concrete plan in place to hasten the process of implementation. Then take the right steps and actions to assist and accelerate the process of implementation.

➢ **Initiatives worksheet**

Project description	Start/End dates	Outcomes	How the initiative supports goals and/or visions

➢ **Too many or too few projects?**

Having too many projects to do at the same time doesn't signify

success or provide desirable results at the end of the day. Do you

realize you can have as many as a hundred projects and still

experience no satisfaction? The issue isn't about having too many projects, but the ability to pursue these projects and get meaningful results.

Ironically, some of the projects you are interested in do not contribute to your betterment or of the company at large. These projects reflect your misplaced priorities. Any project you want to embark upon that doesn't complement your performance goals or vision is not worth celebrating. It is always beneficial to channel your energy and resources on projects that best describe your ideal dreams and aspirations. It is usually a major setback when organizations fail to identify the projects critically relevant to the growth of the organization.

As an organization or an individual, don't focus on the number of projects. Rather, emphasize the compatibility of the projects to your vision and performance goals. If the projects do not align with your goals, stay away from them.

When projects do not align with goals, the leadership of the company begins to be questioned. A good leader is expected to be realistic, even while taking risks to benefit the organization. A miscalculated risk that appears in the form of a project can mar the smooth operations of the company, impacting multiple situations in the work environment. All this can be avoided when the leaders concentrate on projects beneficial to the development of the company.

Leaders are only able to achieve so much when they are disciplined. Lack of discipline will only cause leaders, and individual staff, to indulge in white elephant projects that will not only consume time, but also impact the financial resources of the company. Of what use is a huge budget when there are no hopes for generating income or expansion? So, leaders are required to play an important role and make big decisions that will assist the company to experience growth and expansion in its operations.

To be a successful leader it is important to pay attention to these questions when faced with multiple projects or tasks in your organizations:

*How will you prioritize these projects?

*Which projects will you cancel or postpone so as to focus your attention?

*Which projects will you delegate to others in your organization?

PROFESSIONAL RELATIONSHIPS

A professional relationship is a mutual interaction between or among various individuals in the same work environment who are governed by ethical standards. The work environment requires various employees and individuals who work together to come to a common understanding of the work environment.

The work environment will not be successful if the professional relationship among various individuals is not in place. It is the bind that connects every individual to some or all the others in the organization. It is the backbone of the organization.

The type of relationship that takes place in the work environment determines the productivity level of the organization. It is only when the individuals in the organization enjoy mutual understanding, engage in positive relationships, and communicate effectively with one another, that they find the work environment enjoyable and, as such, put in their best at work.

Building professional relationships in the work environment requires the willingness of all the individuals involved. There has to be trust, respect, teamwork, and great communication among all the individuals for the relationships to flourish. Additionally, good professional relationships will help you in your career advancement. So, when building a professional relationship in the work environment, you are doing it not only for the benefit of the company, but also for your personal development.

➢ Types of professional relationships

When considering the benefits of professional relationships, it is important to understand the various types of professional relationships in the work environment. They are:

Close-distant relationship: This type of relationship is not entirely real. They exist between individuals who belong to the same industry, but not within the same organization. This professional relationship type is close yet distant. They share similar qualities of being in the same industry but do not have any personal knowledge of each other. Sometimes, the relationship is encouraged with the aid of social media platforms or at social gatherings. In this relationship, both parties benefit from having ties in the industry while being outside of their respective companies.

Semi-close relationships: This is a professional relationship type that encourages communication be among concerned individuals. Though the communication may not be constant, both parties find time to exchange pleasantries whenever they meet or there is a need. In this relationship type, unlike the close-distant relationship, the parties are able to request assistance from each other because they communicate often.

Transactional-based relationship: This is not a close type of relationship. There is no personal relationship whatsoever. This relationship is purely business-related. An example of the transactional-based relationship is one that exists among managers, customers, and suppliers. They accommodate each other solely for the sake of the business.

Trust-centered relationships: This relationship is referred to as the most personal type of relationship. They exist among senior executives and their partners from different organizations. In some cases, this type of relationship also exists between colleagues at work. They are a long-lasting type of professional relationships, and also lead to successful business plans, deals, and ideas. It is the best form of relationship for building positive and productive efforts in the work environment.

Leaders do not exist in isolation. They depend on all levels to reach their goals. It could be subordinates, partners, superiors, even their clients. For any leader to be successful, that leader needs to understand every individual in the workplace is important. However, wise leaders understand they need not trust everyone who comes their way so as to avoid unpleasant situations.

➤ A table on the activities of various roles

The below table will help you identify the various individuals who contribute, or can contribute, to your success and productivity in the work environment. On the column where "role" is written, it can be your peers and colleagues, mentors, customers, managers, direct reports, other advisors, investors, and other key people. Fill in the name of the person or people in that category. Then, complete the chart by indicating the type of relationship and how this person can help your organization, and you, personally.

ROLE	Type of relationship	How does/can this person help or hinder me
Peers and Colleagues		
Mentors		
Customers		
Managers		
Direct Reports		
Investors		
Outside advisors/coaches		
Other key people		

PILLAR THREE

PROFESSIONAL DEVELOPMENT

Professional development is essential for an individual who wants to improve. It is an avenue where you get to develop and acquire specialized skills. Learning is a continuous process and as such, you can never stop learning.

It may require formal education, but this is not entirely compulsory. Aside from formal education, you can acquire professional development by watching other people perform a certain task and learning from their experience. Professional development skills include learning technical skills, doing personal branding, foresting collaboration, using strategic thinking methods to succeed, implementing careful time management, and executing timely project management. It is almost impossible for you to get all the relevant skills in the work environment. But, as long as you are willing to learn, it is possible to be better than you ever thought possible. The secret to this is to avail yourself whenever the opportunity comes your way.

As a leader, encourage your staff to favor professional development. If you possess the capacity to help your staff develop their skills or education, assist them in whatever way you can. Always encourage them. When your staff possesses the necessary experience, skills, and education, they perform better and propel the growth of the organization.

There are various examples of professional development. They include:

Professional development education program: This program is essential in ensuring you get the necessary education that will be relevant to the job.

Executive Coaching Programs: Besides formal professional training, executive coaching is an excellent one on one option for growth of the organization and the leader being coached.

Coaching is one of the only leadership development solutions that provides human-to-human support over time. A coach's primary roles is to help you explore your own thoughts, assumptions, and blind spots through powerful conversation.

Working with a coach brings focus, clarity, and structure to professional development, delivering increased insight, achieving measurable, and group potentials, and personal intangible results.

Training programs: Make yourself available for programs aimed at instilling the right skills and knowledge essential for the position you have assumed.

Some examples of training programs are:

- Attending seminars

- Attending conferences

- Participating in online testing

Research: You need to find out new things on your own. The internet has made many provisions for training. Aside from the internet, you can also make it a habit to read books. There are secrets embedded in the pages of books. The answer you need is somewhere within your reach, grasp it.

Job performance: This is one very important way of developing your professional skills and talents. Set limits you wish to attain. Do not be afraid to try new things and set big goals. If your set goals for this week were easily achievable, set bigger goals for next week, and work towards achieving them, too.

Consider your vision, mission, values, performance goals, and initiatives. What will it take for you to succeed? What strengths can you build on? What behaviors will you need to adopt or modify? What knowledge and/or skills will you need to acquire?

If your answer is "none" then go back and set some more challenging goals, or create a more aspirational and outrageous vision that will inspire and motivate you and your employees. When you feel your goals have become a stretch for you, then fill in the following worksheets:

Strengths Worksheet:

List one to three strengths you can build upon to achieve your goals and vision.

Strength	How it supports my goals and vision	How can I build on this strength to be even more effective

Behaviors Worksheet:

List one to three behaviors you can change to achieve your performance goals and vision.

Old Behavior	How this behavior keeps me from attaining my goals and vision	New behavior: "I will…"

Skills Worksheet:

List three skills or areas of knowledge you need to acquire to be successful

Skill/Area of Knowledge	How it will help me achieve my goals and vision	How and when will I develop

DRAFT AN INITIAL PLAN

Now that you have substantial data from the previous worksheets, it is time to use that work to draft your initial Leadership Plan by summarizing your thoughts and work in the template below :

Area	Plan/statement
Vision	
Mission	
Values	
Performance	
Initiatives	
Professional Relationships (list key names)	
Development	

GET FEEDBACK

You now have a complete Leadership Plan to energize you, your environment, and assist you in taking your position as a leader. Before you conclude this plan is accurate and compelling, check with people whom you respect. Others often see aspects of ourselves we may overlook.

Think about the Professional Relationships whom you have listed. Choose multiple people who you feel you can trust with commenting on this effort. Try to get three to five names, preferably people who work closely with you and understand the overall work environments. If for some reason you cannot use people from your own organization, try trusted friends in your network outside of the organization. If you have an executive coach this may be one person to consider.

Try to have one on one conversations with each of them to review and gain understand of their perspective. The goal in these conversations is to gain a more robust and encompassing view. Be prepared that one or more of these people you bring into your trusted circle may not agree with what you have written. That does not mean you must automatically change things. Acquiring these other perspectives is to give you more data, more insights, and help then narrow blind spots.

Get their feedback by asking:

Area	Plan/statement
Vision	<ul><li>Does my Vision make sense to you?</li><li>Have I pushed myself far enough?</li><li>How can my Vision be more compelling?</li><li>Would others in the organization react to it favorably?</li></ul>
Mission	<ul><li>Does this mission statement seem in line with my vision?</li><li>Does my mission fit with the mission of the company?</li><li>Does this mission seem compelling to you?</li></ul>
Values	<ul><li>From watching me, how would you define my values?</li><li>Does it look like I embody my values?</li><li>How can I improve expressing these values in my work?</li><li>Do my values relate to our company's values?</li></ul>
Performance	<ul><li>Will these goals help me succeed??</li><li>Am I pushing my goals?</li><li>Is each goal specific?</li><li>Will these performance goals help me achieve the above vision?</li></ul>
Initiatives	<ul><li>What three projects of mine would you choose</li></ul>

	to help me achieve my performance goals? • Are there more direct projects I can do? • Are the outcomes specific enough?
Professional Relationships	• Who are the key people I should engage to succeed? • Are the people I have listed the best people? • What advice would you offer to strengthen these relationships?
Development	• What behaviors will help me achieve my performance goals. • What behaviors will help me achieve my vision? • How can I build on my best strengths to achieve my goals

Finalize the Plan and Take Action

With the feedback from three to five of your colleagues, take time to review comments and perspectives. Think about what adaptations you will make to complete your plan. Now actually sit down and update your plan. Keep this document on your desk, pocket, your mobile device or anywhere accessible. Anytime you feel stressed or pulled in too many directions, refer to it. It will help you focus on what really matters at work.

Example plan:

Area	Plan/statement
Vision	To create a business that becomes nationally recognized for its ability to help convicts change their behavior and improve their performance with a simple and powerful process.

Mission	Work becomes a source of fulfillment for everyone. People make the powerful shift achieving goals they never thought possible.
Values	• Be passionate • Be curious • Serve everyone I can...every convict is a potential success story.
Performance	In the next year, increase outreach by at least 20 clients, and 10 speaking engagements. In the following year, increase by 40 clients and be so busy that I can hire additional staff.
Initiatives	• Publish a book on my work by October • Find 20 complementary firms who will exchange referrals by October • Identify. join five associations, June
Professional Relationships	• Each and every client I meet will be a professional relationship
Development	• I will learn about how to self-publish and market a book • I will be less modest about my talents and expertise and evangelize what I do to everyone in the prison marketplace. • In the next year I will learn at least two new assessment tools to use in my practice

CONCLUSION

As a leader, you need to make effective decisions about everything around you. While there are many factors that contribute to your success, as a leader, as a person, one thing is certain; you cannot do it without having come to terms with your personality. You need to understand who you are, and why you are, so you are aligned with your mission and vision.

This is NOT a one-time thing. You MUST keep reviewing, assessing, changing, and adapting to the environment. The environment of your company, of your industry, of the economy, and of your own goals and visions. Yes, over time, your own goals and visions may change and if so, will require another analysis and realignment.

Make it a goal to do this process at least once a year to create your own Assess/Plan/Act repeat cycle of continuous improvement.

The business environment is very competitive, and now, even more strained and thus, hypercompetitive. You can only stay ahead of the competition when you start off on the right footing. How? Put your mission and vision in place. These will help you monitor your performance in the work environment.

You don't need to be limited to the confines of what you know as a leader. Accommodate your subordinates by using the right type of relationship in the work environment. If you want results from others, build sustainable relationships with your colleagues, subordinates, partners, and everyone you work with; the stronger the bond, the better the results. And you are in business for results!

Growth is essential for every leader. You never stop learning. Make it a responsibility to learn something new each and every day, working or rest day. It may be a new skill, training, or even a continuing education program. Whatever form it might take, never stop learning.

Taken together, this approach will make you a leader with a difference. Times are changing, and with once in a hundred year events taking place regularly, you must be ready for the next disaster. The demands of the market are on the rise. You can be on top of your game when you take the right steps. Start today!

Appendix:
YOUR Wheel of Life

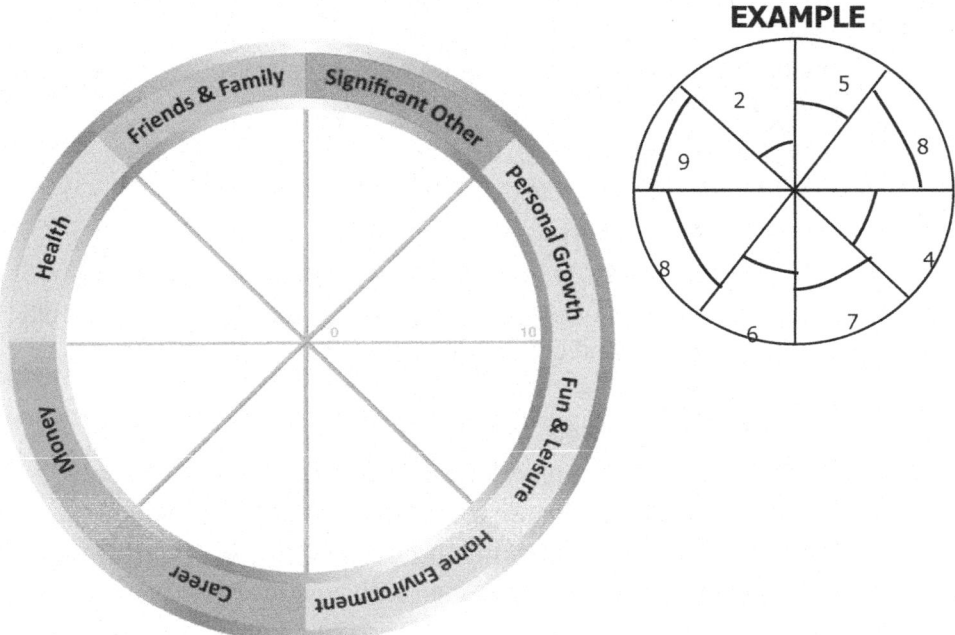

EXAMPLE

COMPLETE THE WHEEL:

1. **Review the 8 Wheel Segments –** think briefly what a satisfying life might look for you in each area.
2. **Next, draw a line across each segment that represents your satisfaction score for each area.**

- Imagine the center of the wheel is 0 and the outer edge is 10.
- Choose a value between 1 (very dissatisfied) and 10 (fully satisfied).
- Now draw a line and write the score alongside (see example above).

The new perimeter of the circle represents your Wheel of Life. "Is it a bumpy ride?"

Now, looking at the wheel, here are some great questions to think about to take this exercise deeper:

1. Are there any surprises for you?
2. How do you feel about your life as you look at your Wheel?
3. How do you *currently* spend time in these areas? How would you *like* to spend time in these areas?
4. What would make that a score of 10?
5. What would a score of 10 look like?
6. Which of these categories would you *most* like to improve?
7. How could you make space for these changes in your life?
8. What help and support might you need from others to make changes and be more satisfied with your life?
9. What change *should* you make first? And what change do you *want* to make first?

   If there was one key action you could take that would begin to bring everything into balance, what would it be?

Lists of core value words:

Integrity	Grace	**Spirituality**
Accountability	Gratitude	Adaptability
Candor	Happiness	Altruism
Commitment	Hope	Balance
Dependability	Inspiring	Charity
Dignity	Irreverent	Communication
Honesty	Joy	Community
Honor	Kindness	Connection
Responsibility	Love	Consciousness
Sincerity	Optimism	Contribution
Transparency	Passion	Cooperation
Trust	Peace	Courtesy
Trustworthy	Poise	Devotion
Truth	Respect	Equality
	Reverence	Ethical
Feelings	Satisfaction	Fairness
Acceptance	Serenity	Family
Comfort	Thankful	Fidelity
Compassion	Tranquility	Friendship
Contentment	Welcoming	Generosity
Empathy		Giving

Goodness

Harmony

Humility

Loyalty

Maturity

Meaning

Selfless

Sensitivity

Service

Sharing

Spirit

Stewardship

Support

Sustainability

Teamwork

Tolerance

Unity

Achievement

Accomplishment

Capable

Challenge

Competence

Credibility

Determination

Development

Drive

Effectiveness

Empower

Endurance

Excellence

Famous

Greatness

Growth

Hard work

Improvement

Influence

Intensity

Leadership

Mastery

Motivation

Performance

Persistence

Potential

Power

Productivity

Prosperity

Recognition

Results-oriented

Risk

Significance

Skill

Skillfulness

Status

Success

Talent

Victory

Wealth

Winning

Creativity

Creation

Curiosity

Discovery

Exploration

Expressive

Imagination

Innovation

Inquisitive

Intuitive

Openness

Originality

Uniqueness

Wonder

Enjoyment

Amusement

Enthusiasm

Experience

Fun

Humor

Playfulness

Recreation

Spontaneous

Surprise

Presence

Alertness

Attentive

Awareness

Beauty

Calm

Clear

Concentration

Focus

Silence

Simplicity

Solitude

Intelligence

Brilliance

Clever

Common sense

Decisiveness

Foresight

Genius

Insightful

Knowledge

Learning

Logic

Openness

Realistic

Reason

Reflective

Smart

Thoughtful

Vision

Wisdom

Strength

Ambition

Assertiveness

Boldness

Confidence

Dedication

Discipline

Ferocious

Fortitude

Persistence

Power

Restraint

Rigor

Self-reliance

Temperance

Toughness

Vigor

Will

Freedom

Independence

Individuality

Liberty

Courage

Bravery	Cleanliness	Security
Conviction	Consistency	Stability
Fearless	Control	Structure
Valor	Decisive	Thorough
	Economy	Timeliness
Order	Justice	
Accuracy	Lawful	**Health**
Careful	Moderation	Energy
Certainty	Organization	Vitality

AUTHOR'S BIOGRAPHY

Jim Saliba has thirty plus years' experience working in the technology and software industries, encountering just about every issue a leader might face. Jim takes his years of experience and observations to share winning insider activities to drive your leadership, while becoming "unstuck" from the overwhelming challenges that hold us back from business success.

Jim holds a BS degree in Computer Systems, and an MBA, along with several industry certifications. He is a professional leadership coach, and worldwide speaker based in San Jose, California. You can find Jim coaching, training, and mentoring leaders across many industries, or, in his wood shop handcrafting wooden toys for his grandsons.